CONTENTS

About the Author 1

Introduction 2

Planning Your Appliqué Quilt 2
Selecting Your Blocks 2
Setting Your Blocks 2
Choosing Your Fabric 6
Assembling Your Supplies 6
Making Paper Patterns 7
Making Appliqué Templates 7
Cutting Appliqué Pieces 7
Choosing an Appliqué Technique 7

Rose of Sharon Wreath 8
Wallhanging One 10
Wallhanging Two 15
Petunia Wreath 24
Scrappy Tulips 26
Christmas Cheer 29

©2013, from *Easy Floral Appliqué Patterns* (AQS, 2003)

About the Author...

"It seems like I was born with a needle in my hand," says Eula Mae Long. She loved sewing so much that, in high school, she took four years of it in home economics. Then, while her children were in school, she took every sewing class the adult education system gave, including a nine-month power sewing class.

Next came a clothing color and design class at a junior college, which proved helpful for choosing colors when she began quilting. She first tried her hand at quilting when her grandchild was born. Eula Mae says, "The stitches in that Sunbonnet Sue and Overall Bill quilt had what we call 'toe catcher' stitches, but it lasted until grandson Chuck was about 10 years old."

On a cruise with the late Doreen Speckman, she discovered appliqué in a class taught by Nancy Pearson. Eula Mae has been quilting and taking quilt classes ever since. Along the way, she began teaching quilting with her good friend, Irma Woody. Then she discovered that she loved making her own appliqué designs. Others enjoyed her designs and encouraged her to share them with quilters.

Introduction

This book is dedicated to the members of my quilt group, but truly, I have to say the inspiration came from some women I talked to at a quilt show in Wichita, Kansas. I had tired feet, so I sat down to rest, and it wasn't long until about six other quilters were resting, too. We began discussing our favorite subject … appliqué. There were few appliqué quilts in this beautiful show, which started the women talking about what types of designs they liked to sew. They didn't want folk art patterns or the beautiful Baltimore-type appliqué, which had so many little pieces to handle. What they wanted were more modern designs, especially flowers, with large pieces that were easy to see and easy to handle. A quilt teacher in the group said she believed that beginning and intermediate appliquérs had few designs to choose from, especially if they lived in small towns.

I went home to Nebraska, where I lived at that time, and I dwelled on this problem and realized how true those women's words were. We needed more designs that would appeal to the average appliquér. So my job of designing began. Since my love of flowers comes close to my love of appliqué, the job was more joy than work, especially because I've been designing most of my own appliqué quilts for some time.

So enjoy, and may your days be filled with appliqué.

Planning your Appliqué Quilt

Selecting Your Blocks

Once you have looked over the photographs and patterns, you have some decisions to make before you make a mad rush to a fabric shop or start digging through your many boxes of scraps.

What block or blocks have you decided to use for your project? You can choose one block and repeat it to make a whole quilt or choose several designs to make a modern sampler quilt. Another option is to make a large central design, such as a large basket of flowers, and select blocks to go around it, medallion-style.

Whatever you choose, make a sample of each of your chosen blocks before you go any further with the whole project. A sample block will give you a better idea of what colors you do and don't want in your project. Be sure to balance the color in your appliqué pieces. For example, if you put a yellow flower on one side of the basket, try to have a yellow flower on the opposite side. In addition, you can change the shapes of the leaves or reposition them. You can change the flowers, too, and why not? It's your project. You can also change the size of the patterns if you want a larger or smaller block. A good photocopy machine will do the job.

Setting Your Blocks

How are you going to put your blocks together? Look over the diagrams on page 3 for ideas. Blocks can be set block to block, alternated with plain blocks, sewn together with setting strips, or set in many more ways.

If you are making a bed quilt, you have a variety of settings to choose from. In some of the settings, there is room for a large central design. To help you plan your bed-sized quilt, refer to the Quilt Sizes chart on page 4. You can choose borders in widths and colors to complete the size you need and the look you want for your quilt.

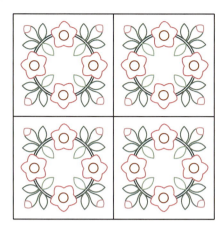

FIG. 1. BLOCKS SET SIDE BY SIDE

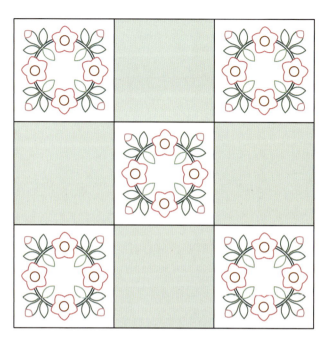

FIG. 2. APPLIQUÉ BLOCKS SET WITH ALTERNATE PLAIN BLOCKS

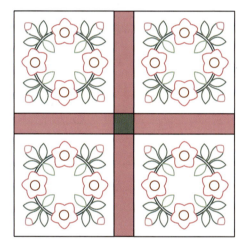

FIG. 3. BLOCKS SET WITH SASHING STRIPS

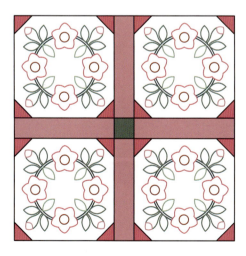

FIG. 4. BLOCKS SET WITH CORNER TRIANGLES AND SASHING

For an on-point setting, use the Diagonal Sets table on page 5 to help you figure out how many blocks you will need. For example, a 14" block set on point is approximately 20" across, from corner to corner.

On-point blocks require setting triangles for the sides and corners of the quilt. To create the side triangles, cut a fabric square that is at least 1¼" larger than your block's diagonal measurement. Cut the square diagonally twice to yield four side triangles. For the corner triangles, cut a fabric square that is at least ⅞" larger than half your block's diagonal measurement. Cut the square diagonally once to produce two corner triangles.

Planning Your Appliqué Quilt

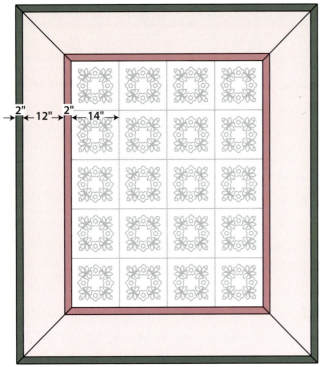

Setting A. Twenty blocks set straight with multiple plain borders

Bed Quilt Sizes

Bed	Mattress size	Quilt size
Twin	38" x 75"	68" x 105"
Double	54" x 75"	84" x 105"
Queen	60" x 80"	90" x 110"
King	76" x 80"	106" x 110"
California king	72" x 84"	102" x 114"

These sizes allow for a 15" drop on all sides.

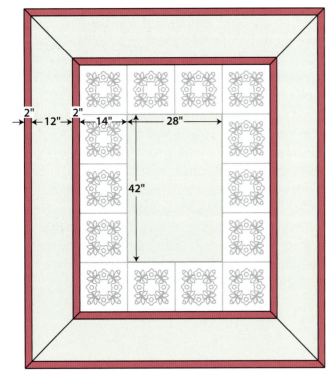

Setting B. Fourteen blocks set around a rectangular center, with multiple plain borders

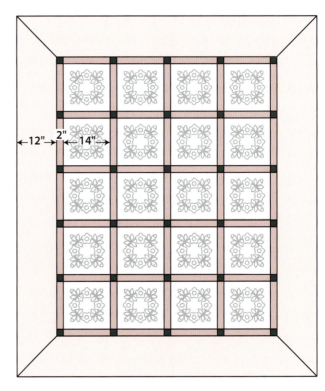

Setting C. Twenty blocks set straight with sashing and plain border

Planning Your Appliqué Quilt

4 APPLIQUÉ GARDEN   Eula Mae Long

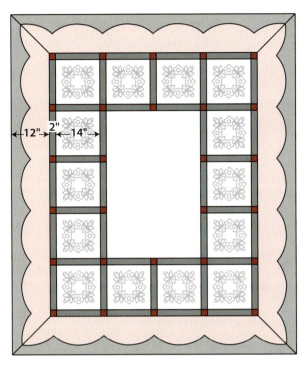

Setting D. Fourteen blocks set straight with sashing, rectangular center, and swag border

Diagonal Sets

Block Size	Diagonal
8"	11⅜"
10"	14⅛"
12"	17"
14"	19⅞"
15"	21¼"
16"	22⅝"

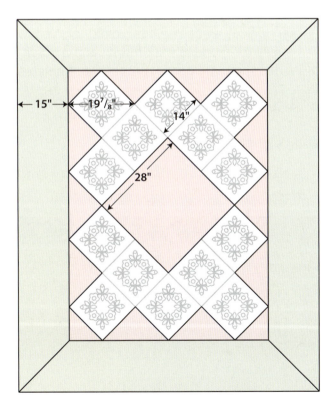

Setting E. Fourteen blocks set on point around a square center, with plain border

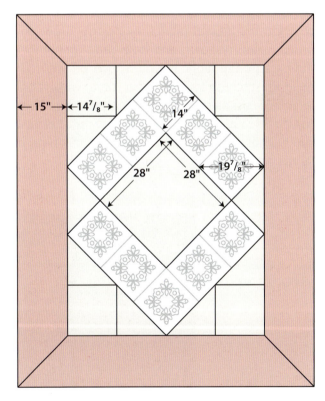

Setting F. Ten blocks set on point around a square center, with four corner blocks

Planning Your Appliqué Quilt

APPLIQUÉ GARDEN · Eula Mae Long · 5

Choosing Your Fabric

Your fabric choices are important when making a quilt or any fabric project. If you are a beginner, I suggest that you pick a small flowered print that has several of the colors you like. We will call this your "theme fabric." Then pick a palette of fabrics with colors that are in your theme fabric. Choose shades from light to dark in each color. Don't use all plain fabric because your design will be flat with no life. Add dyed fabric, tiny flowers, textured fabrics, and batiks. These will make your design come alive. It's the same with leaf fabrics. Choose many greens, and don't forget to turn the fabric over. Many times you can use the wrong side. Fasten swatches of your selected fabrics to a note card to serve as your fabric reference (fig. 5). Most importantly, buy 100 percent cotton fabric and prewash.

What you buy for the background is just as important as your appliqué fabric. Be sure it is 100 percent cotton and prewash it. There are many beautiful types of fabrics to choose from. If you select muslin, get the best quality because low-quality muslin shrinks a lot. There are many colors in marbleized fabrics, and don't forget tiny prints, dainty yellows, and pale gray. Remember, the background fabric is what shows off your tiny quilting stitches, so take your time with fabric selection. Pass on stiff fabric, no matter how pretty it is. Also be cautious of loosely woven fabric because you will lose your quilting stitches in this type of fabric.

Assembling Your Supplies

Once you have chosen your fabrics, you will need to assemble the following supplies:

- Tracing paper

- Template plastic

- Scissors: one pair for fabric, one pair for paper, and one small, sharp, pointed pair for appliqué

- Thread: white 100 percent cotton for basting, and colors to match the fabric pieces for appliqué. If there is no match, go slightly darker.

- Needles: size 10–12

- Pins and pincushion

- Thimble

- Marking pencils: a sharp #2 or fine-pointed mechanical pencil; white, pink, or yellow pencils for marking dark fabric; and a black-leaded template pencil for making templates

- Seam ripper

- Iron and ironing board

HIGH-CONTRAST PRINTS CAN PRODUCE DRAMATIC BLOCKS.

FIG. 5. SAMPLE THEME FABRIC PALETTE

- Rotary cutter
- Freezer paper, if desired for appliqué
- Directional lamp
- Sewing machine

Making Paper Patterns

Take extra care in tracing the design you have chosen for your project onto paper. An accurate pattern will make your project easier to sew. For tracing patterns, I suggest you get a large pad of tracing paper from an art store. On a sheet of this paper, mark your 14" square and cut it out. Then fold this square in half horizontally and vertically and mark the creases with dotted lines (fig. 6). Place the paper square over the pattern in the book and trace the design, keeping the dotted lines on your tracing paper properly positioned with the lines in the book. Then go over the traced lines with a black felt-tip pen. Now you have a paper pattern that can be used over and over to trace the designs on the background fabric (fig. 7).

Transfer the pattern to your background squares as follows: If your background fabric is light colored, all you need to do is tape your tracing paper pattern on a sheet of white poster board. Place the background fabric over the pattern, and use a fine-point mechanical pencil to trace the lines. If you draw slightly inside the pattern lines, the appliqué pieces will cover the lines. If the fabric is too dark to see the pattern through it, you will need a light source, such as a window or light table.

Making Appliqué Templates

With a black template pencil or a sharp lead pencil, trace the appliqué pattern pieces onto clear plastic template material. Make a template for every appliqué piece in the block. Do not add seam allowances to the appliqué templates.

Write on every template piece any placement numbers, grain line marks, and the name of the pattern. Place all template pieces in a small, zipper-sealed plastic bag. Mark the plastic bag with the name of the project.

Cutting Appliqué Pieces

Place the template on the right side of the fabric. With a fine-line or very sharp pencil, mark around the template. Leave about ½" of space between tracings. When you are cutting out the appliqué patches, add a ¼" seam allowance by eye. This seam allowance will be the turn-under for the appliqué patch. The appliqué patches can be stored in the plastic bag with the templates.

Choosing an Appliqué Technique

There are many ways to appliqué. If you have a special technique you like, why change it? If you are a beginner, it's best to try many methods. Taking appliqué classes is a great way to learn these methods. When you find one that you really feel comfortable with, stay with it and practice, practice, and practice some more. I suggest doing some type of appliqué at least twice a week or more. As the old saying goes, "Practice makes perfect."

You will notice that some of the patterns have numbered pieces to let you know in what order the pieces are to be appliquéd. To reduce bulk, do not turn under the allowances where one piece fits underneath another.

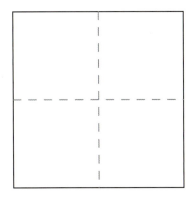

Fig. 6. Prepare a 14" square of the tracing paper.

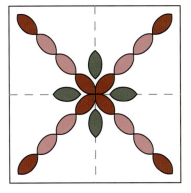

Fig. 7. To trace, align the vertical and horizontal lines with the pattern.

Rose of Sharon Wreath

ROSE OF SHARON WREATH
20½" x 20½", wallhanging made by the author

PLACEMENT DIAGRAM

Grid squares represent 3". Use bias tube for stem circle. Appliqué the flowers in the order in which real flowers grow: stems, leaves, flowers.

bud tip
cut 4

bud
cut 4

leaf
cut 12

flower
cut 4

flower center
cut 4

For turned-edge appliqué techniques, add ¼" turn-under allowances, by eye, as you cut your fabric pieces.

APPLIQUÉ GARDEN

Rose of Sharon Wreath

Eula Mae Long

Wallhanging One

Wallhanging One

39" x 39", contains Dyana's Daisy, Tania's Tulips, Oregon Beauty, and Cotton Candy

Wall quilt, pieced by the author and machine quilted by Marie Warden, Salem, Oregon

Dyana's Daisy

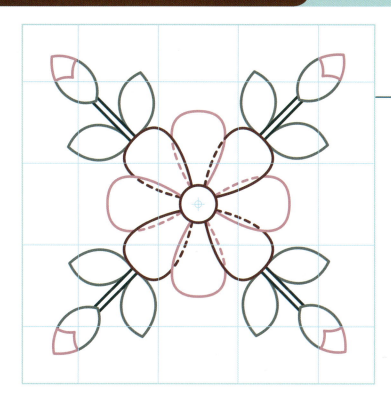

Placement Diagram

Grid squares represent 3". Stems are made with bias tubes. Appliqué the flowers in the order in which real flowers grow: stems, leaves, flowers.

Full-sized patterns on this page for 14" block.

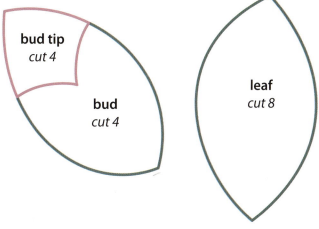

bud tip
cut 4

bud
cut 4

leaf
cut 8

petal
cut 8

flower center
cut 1

For turned-edge appliqué techniques, add ¼" turn-under allowances, by eye, as you cut your fabric pieces.

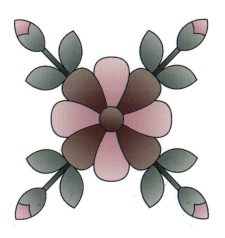

APPLIQUÉ GARDEN

Wallhanging One

Eula Mae Long

Wallhanging One: Tania's Tulip

Placement Diagram

Grid squares represent 3". Stems are made with bias tubes. Appliqué the flowers in the order in which real flowers grow: stems, leaves, flowers.

Full-sized patterns on this page for 14" block.

flower 1 petal 1 — cut 4
flower 1 center — cut 4
flower 1 petal 2 — cut 4
leaf — cut 8
flower 2 — cut 1
flower 2 center — cut 1

For turned-edge appliqué techniques, add ¼" turn-under allowances, by eye, as you cut your fabric pieces.

Wallhanging One: Oregon Beauty

Placement Diagram

Grid squares represent 3". Stems are made with bias tubes. Appliqué the flowers in the order in which real flowers grow: stems, leaves, flowers.

Full-sized patterns on this page for 14" block.

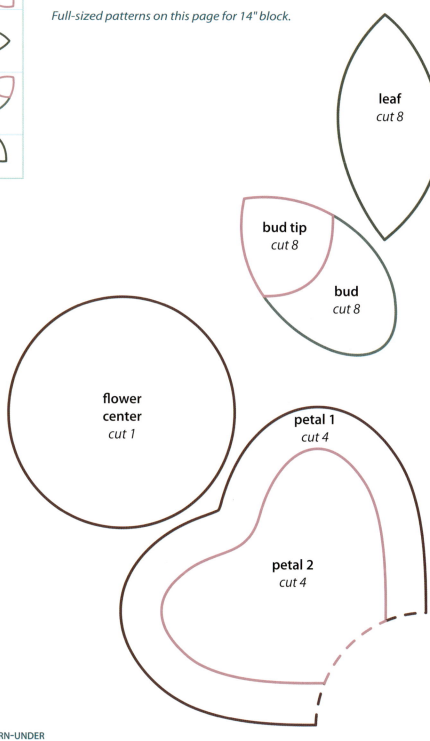

For turned-edge appliqué techniques, add ¼" turn-under allowances, by eye, as you cut your fabric pieces.

APPLIQUÉ GARDEN — Eula Mae Long — 13

Wallhanging One: Cotton Candy

Placement Diagram

Grid squares represent 3". Stems are made with bias tubes. Appliqué the flowers in the order in which real flowers grow: stems, leaves, flowers.

Full-sized patterns on this page for 14" block.

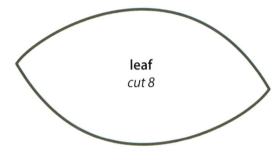

leaf
cut 8

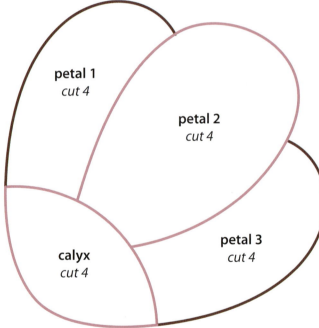

petal 1
cut 4

petal 2
cut 4

petal 3
cut 4

calyx
cut 4

For turned-edge appliqué techniques, add ¼" turn-under allowances, by eye, as you cut your fabric pieces.

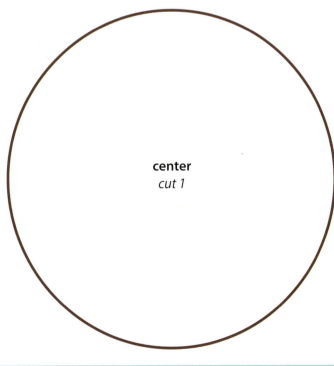

center
cut 1

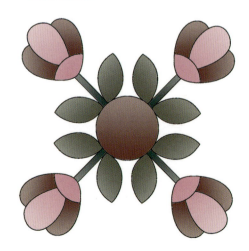

Wallhanging One

14 Appliqué Garden

Eula Mae Long

Wallhanging Two

WALLHANGING TWO

36" x 36", contains Heart of Flowers, Basket of Flowers, Basket of Clematis, and Twirling Tulips, wall quilt, pieced by the author and quilted by Marie Warden, Salem, Oregon, block patterns on pages 16–23

Wallhanging Two: Heart of Flowers

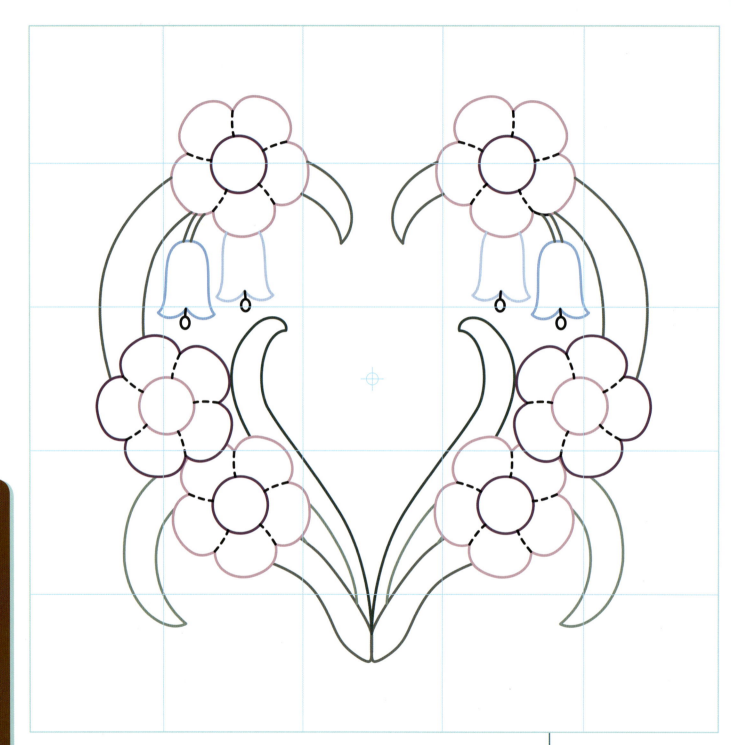

Placement Diagram

Grid squares represent 3". Stems are made with bias tubes. Appliqué the flowers in the order in which real flowers grow: stems, leaves, flowers.

Full-sized patterns on page 17 for 14" block.

Wallhanging Two

16   APPLIQUÉ GARDEN   Eula Mae Long

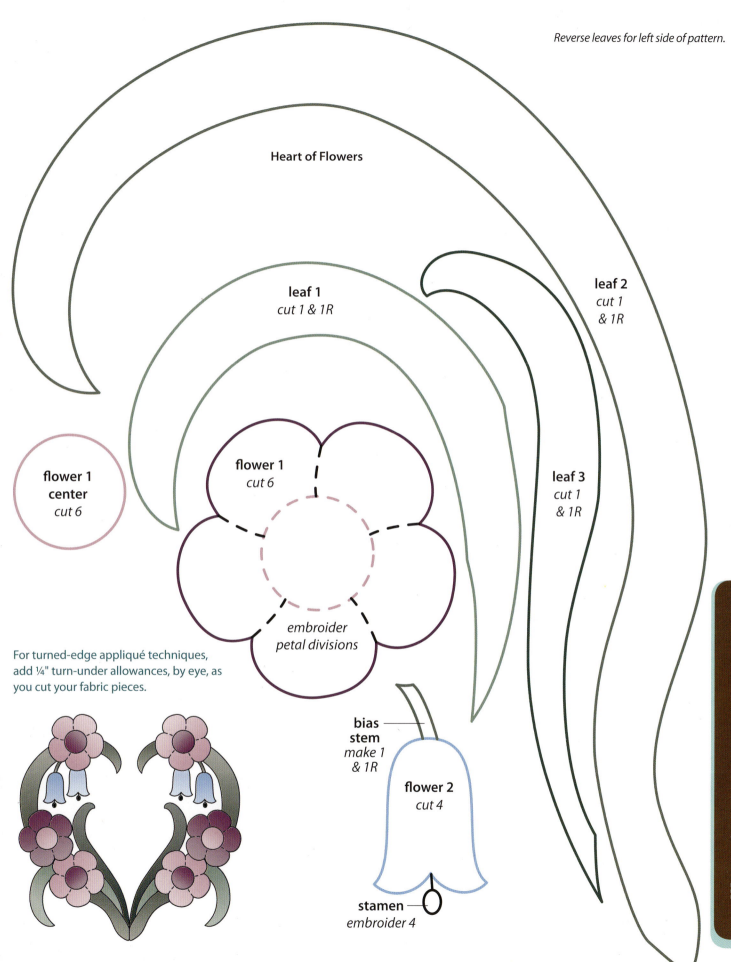

Wallhanging Two: Basket of Clematis

PLACEMENT DIAGRAM

Grid squares represent 3". Appliqué the flowers in the order in which real flowers grow: stems, leaves, flowers.

Full-sized patterns on pages 19 - 20 for 14" block.

Wallhanging Two

18 APPLIQUÉ GARDEN   Eula Mae Long

Wallhanging Two: Basket of Clematis

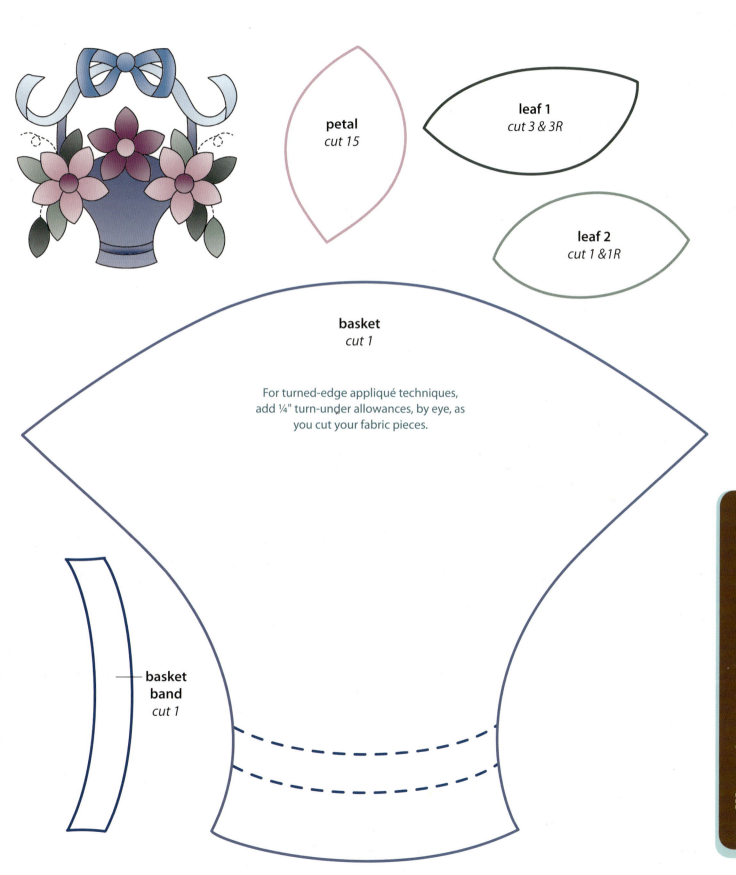

APPLIQUÉ GARDEN

Eula Mae Long

19

Wallhanging Two: Basket of Clematis

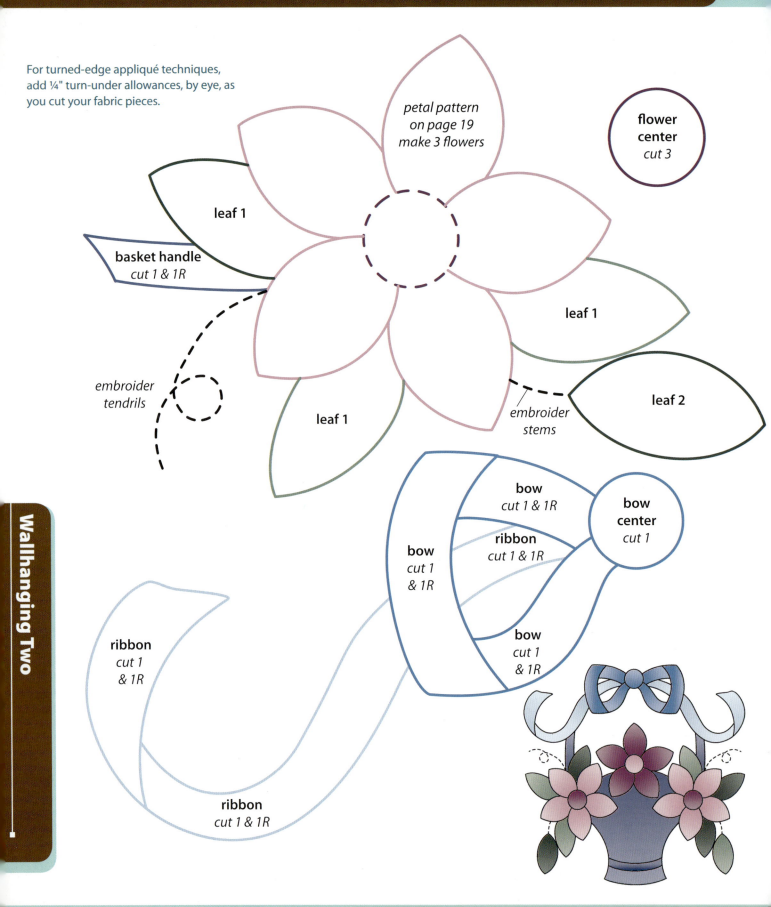

Wallhanging Two: Basket of Flowers

Placement Diagram

Grid squares represent 3". Appliqué the flowers in the order in which real flowers grow: stems, leaves, flowers.

Full-sized patterns on page 22 for 14" block.

APPLIQUÉ GARDEN

Wallhanging Two: Basket of Flowers

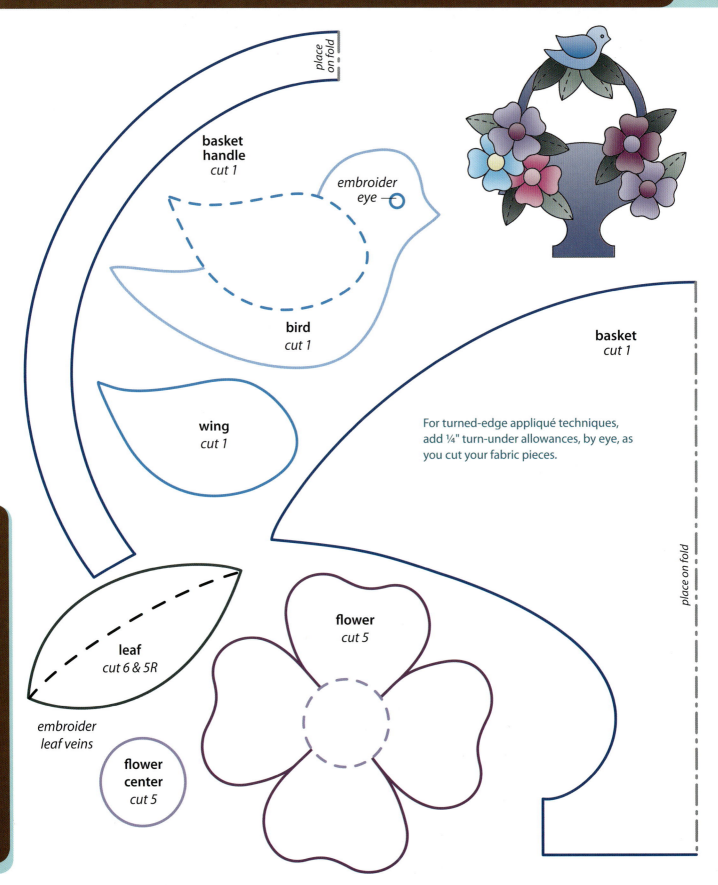

22 APPLIQUÉ GARDEN Eula Mae Long

Wallhanging Two: Twirling Tulips

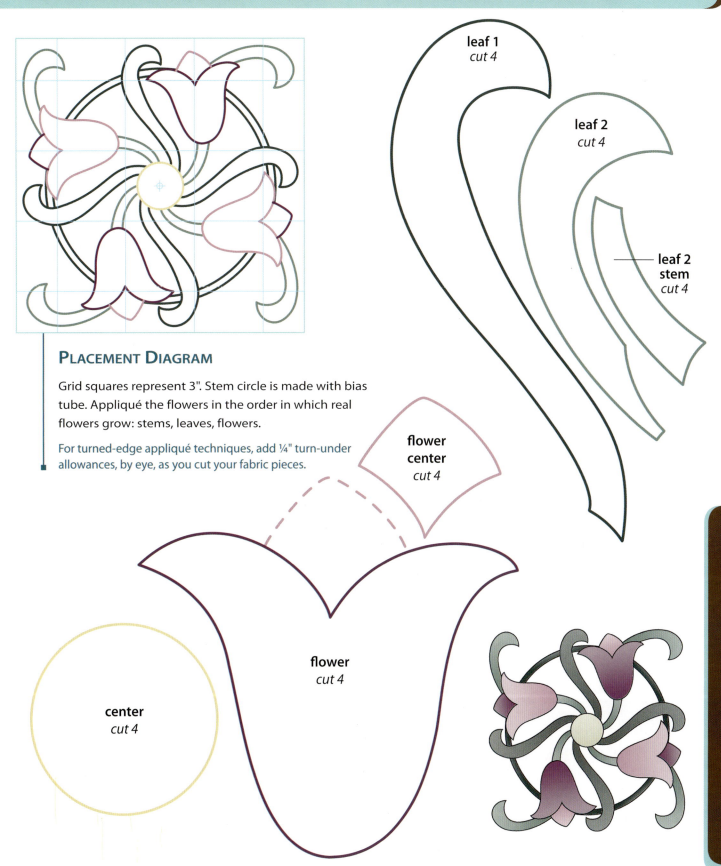

Placement Diagram

Grid squares represent 3". Stem circle is made with bias tube. Appliqué the flowers in the order in which real flowers grow: stems, leaves, flowers.

For turned-edge appliqué techniques, add ¼" turn-under allowances, by eye, as you cut your fabric pieces.

leaf 1 cut 4

leaf 2 cut 4

leaf 2 stem cut 4

flower center cut 4

flower cut 4

center cut 4

Appliqué Garden — Eula Mae Long

Petunia Wreath

Petunia Wreath
84" x 100", bed quilt, pieced by the author and hand quilted by Edna Buhler, Salem, Oregon, block patterns on page 25

Petunia Wreath

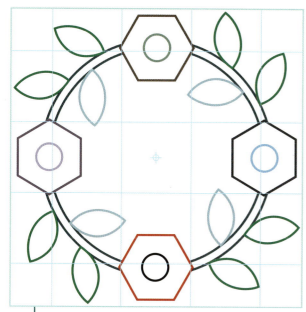

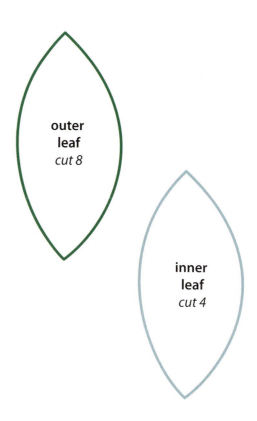

outer leaf
cut 8

inner leaf
cut 4

Placement Diagram

Grid squares represent 3". Stems are made with bias tubes. Appliqué the flowers in the order in which real flowers grow: stems, leaves, flowers.

For turned-edge appliqué techniques, add ¼" turn-under allowances, by eye, as you cut your fabric pieces.

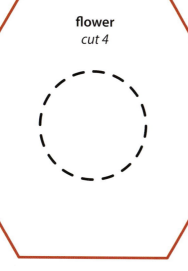

flower center
cut 4

flower
cut 4

APPLIQUÉ GARDEN

Eula Mae Long 25

SCRAPPY TULIPS

SCRAPPY TULIPS
84" x 100", bed quilt, pieced by the author and hand quilted by Edna Buhler, Salem, Oregon, block patterns on page 27

APPLIQUÉ GARDEN

Scrappy Tulips

Placement Diagram

Grid squares represent 3". Stems are made with bias tubes. Appliqué the flowers in the order in which real flowers grow: stems, leaves, flowers.

For turned-edge appliqué techniques, add ¼" turn-under allowances, by eye, as you cut your fabric pieces.

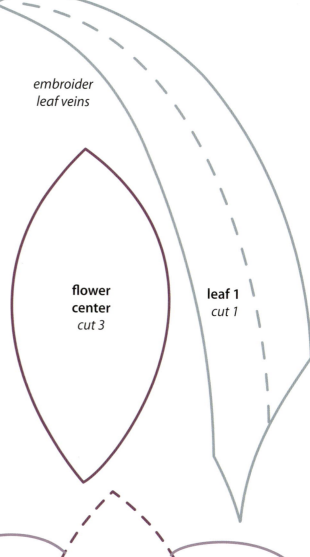

embroider leaf veins

flower center *cut 3*

leaf 1 *cut 1*

flower *cut 3*

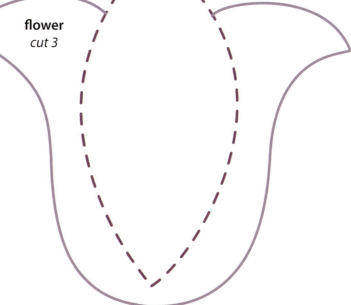

APPLIQUÉ GARDEN
Eula Mae Long 27

Scrappy Tulips

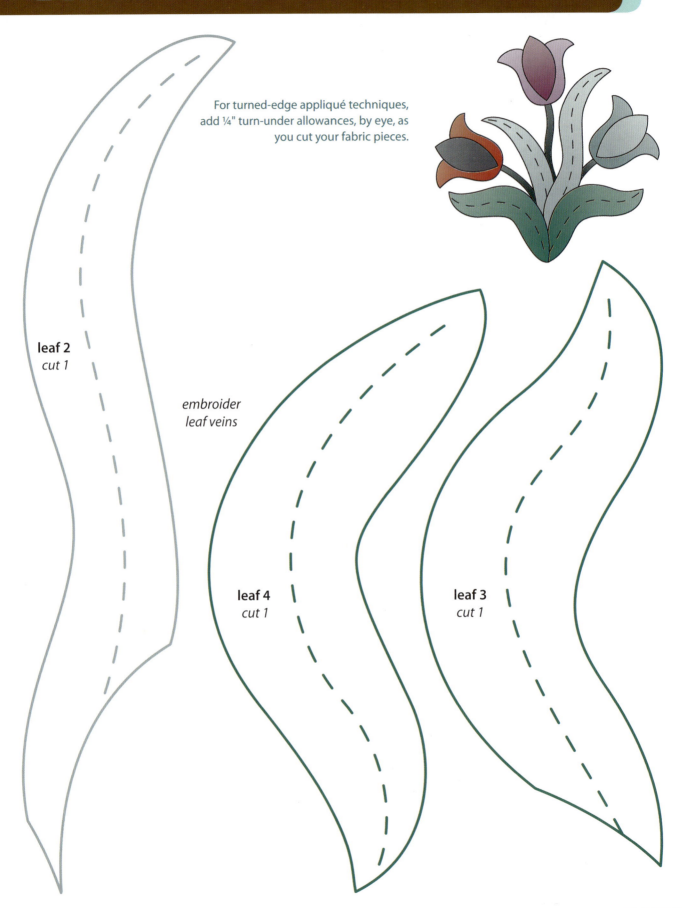

For turned-edge appliqué techniques, add ¼" turn-under allowances, by eye, as you cut your fabric pieces.

leaf 2
cut 1

embroider leaf veins

leaf 4
cut 1

leaf 3
cut 1

28 APPLIQUÉ GARDEN Eula Mae Long

Christmas Cheer

CHRISTMAS CHEER

84" x 98", bed quilt, pieced by the author and machine quilted by Quilt and Stitch Shop, Slayton, Oregon

Christmas Cheer: Christmas Block

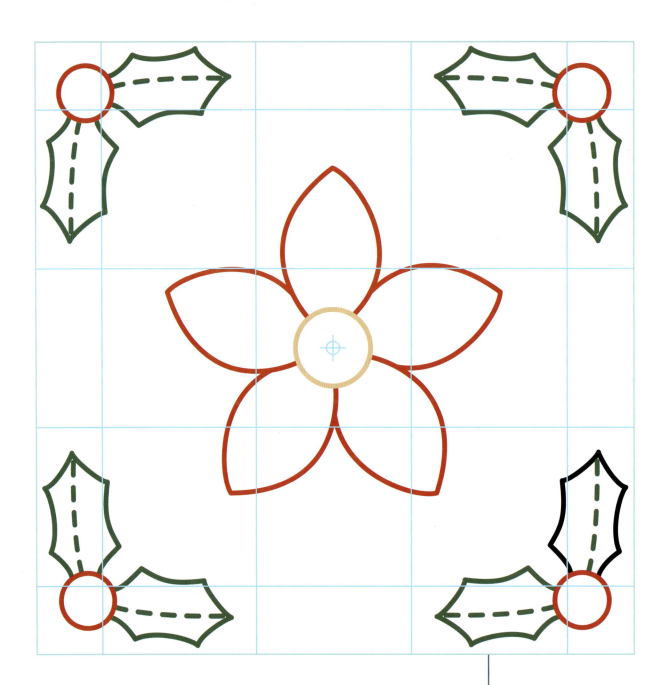

PLACEMENT DIAGRAM

Grid squares represent 3". Appliqué the flowers in the order in which real flowers grow: leaves then flowers.

Full-sized patterns on page 31 for 14" block.

Christmas Cheer

30　APPLIQUÉ GARDEN　　　　　　　　　　　　　　　　　　　Eula Mae Long

Christmas Cheer: Christmas Block

For turned-edge appliqué techniques, add ¼" turn-under allowances, by eye, as you cut your fabric pieces.

petal pattern
make 1 flower

flower center
cut 1

leaf
cut 4 & 4R

embroider leaf veins

flower petal
cut 5

leaf
cut 4 & 4R

berry
cut 4

Christmas Cheer

APPLIQUÉ GARDEN

More AQS Books

This is only a small selection of the books available from the American Quilter's Society. AQS books are known worldwide for timely topics, clear writing, beautiful color photos, and accurate illustrations and patterns. The following books are available from your local bookseller, quilt shop, or public library.

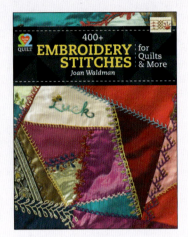
#1274

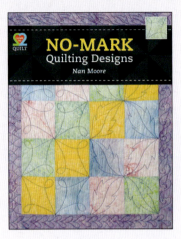
#1277

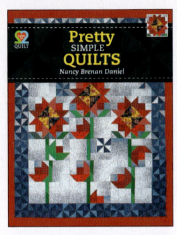
#1278

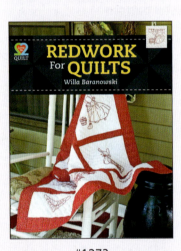
#1273

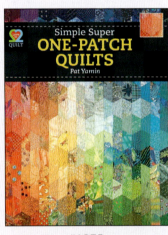
#1275

#1281

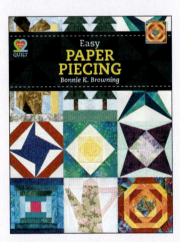
#1279

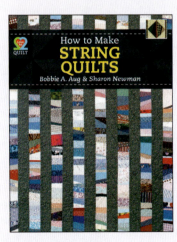
#1282

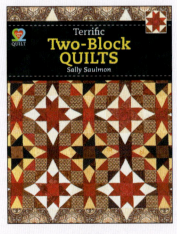
#1283

LOOK for these books nationally.
CALL or **VISIT** our website at

1-800-626-5420
www.AmericanQuilter.com